DUE
PROCESS

MATT BOUGIE

Cavendish
Square

New York

Published in 2018 by Cavendish Square Publishing, LLC
243 5th Avenue, Suite 136, New York, NY 10016

Copyright © 2018 by Cavendish Square Publishing, LLC

First Edition

No part of this publication may be reproduced, stored in a retrieval system, or transmitted in any form or by any means—electronic, mechanical, photocopying, recording, or otherwise—without the prior permission of the copyright owner. Request for permission should be addressed to Permissions, Cavendish Square Publishing, 243 5th Avenue, Suite 136, New York, NY 10016. Tel (877) 980-4450; fax (877) 980-4454.

Website: cavendishsq.com

This publication represents the opinions and views of the author based on his or her personal experience, knowledge, and research. The information in this book serves as a general guide only. The author and publisher have used their best efforts in preparing this book and disclaim liability rising directly or indirectly from the use and application of this book.

All websites were available and accurate when this book was sent to press.

Library of Congress Cataloging-in-Publication Data

Names: Bougie, Matt, author.
Title: Due process / Matt Bougie.
Description: New York : Cavendish Square Publishing, [2018] | Series: Civic values | Includes index.
Identifiers: LCCN 2017029667 (print) | LCCN 2017031408 (ebook) | ISBN 9781502631855 (E-book) | ISBN 9781502631824 (pbk.) | ISBN 9781502631831 (6 pack) | ISBN 9781502631848 (library bound)
Subjects: LCSH: Due process of law--United States. | Civil rights--United States. | United States. Constitution. 5th Amendment. | United States. Constitution. 14th Amendment.
Classification: LCC KF4765 (ebook) | LCC KF4765 .B68 2018 (print) | DDC 347.73/5--dc23
LC record available at https://lccn.loc.gov/2017029667

Editorial Director: David McNamara
Editor: Kristen Susienka
Copy Editor: Rebecca Rohan
Associate Art Director: Amy Greenan
Designer: Alan Sliwinski
Production Coordinator: Karol Szymczuk
Photo Research: J8 Media

The photographs in this book are used by permission and through the courtesy of: Cover ©iStockphoto.com/RichLegg; p. 4 ©iStockphoto.com/PeopleImages; p. 6 View Apart/Shutterstock.com; p. 7 Moodboard/Brand X Pictures/Getty Images; p. 9 Chris Ryan/OJO Images/Getty Images; p. 10 Photos.com/Thinkstock; p.12 ©iStockphoto.com/Sergeyussr; pp. 13, 26 Bettmann/Getty Images; p. 14 ©iStockphoto.com/Leezsnow; pp. 16, 23 MPI/Archive Photos/Getty Images; p. 18 Alex Wong/Getty Images; p. 19 Hero Images/Getty Images; p. 20 Fine Art/Corbis Historical/Getty Images; p. 22 GraphicaArtis/Archive Photos/Getty Images; p. 24 Yana Paskova/Getty Images; p. 27 ValeStock/Shutterstock.com; p. 28 Aneese/Shutterstock.com.

Printed in the United States of America

CONTENTS

Lawyers help people understand how laws work. They are a part of due process.

UNDERSTANDING DUE PROCESS

In the United States, rules and laws help people stay safe and happy. **Civic values** are ideas that people follow to be good citizens. Some examples of civic values are honesty, trust, and respect.

In the United States, everyone has rights, too. Citizen's rights are called **civil rights**. Some examples of civil rights are the right to equality and the right to being protected from **discrimination**. Everyone's rights are protected by something called due process.

In the United States, all people deserve to be treated fairly under the law.

How Due Process Works

Due process is a series of steps that protects people's rights. Every single person is treated the same under the law. This protects people from getting in trouble for things they didn't do. It also means you are treated fairly if you get in trouble. We need due process to make sure everyone's civil rights are protected.

Due process is often used when someone is accused of a crime. At

"The liberties of none are safe unless the liberties of all are protected." —William O. Douglas

first, the person is not punished right away. People called lawyers help them. They let a person tell their

Due process helps protect people's rights, like a bodyguard protects people from harm.

IT BEGAN IN ENGLAND

Due process has a long history. It first started in England. Before someone was punished, he or she had to go through different steps. These steps made sure the person was being treated fairly. These steps also helped make sure the person was not punished for a crime they didn't commit.

side of the story. This is a part of due process. Due process also means police and detectives have to collect information about a crime fairly. They then show that information in court to a judge or jury. The

"No person shall be held to answer for a capital, or otherwise infamous crime, unless on a presentment or indictment of a grand jury ... nor be deprived of life, liberty, or property, without due process of law." —Fifth Amendment (abridged)

Putting someone in jail is very serious. People follow the steps of due process to try and make sure guilty people are punished and innocent people are free.

jury decides if a person is innocent or guilty. A judge decides what punishment is appropriate.

In the United States, due process is very important. It helps to prove whether people are guilty or innocent. It is not always easy. Some steps are very hard.

King John of England signed the Magna Carta in 1215.

CHAPTER TWO

HISTORY OF DUE PROCESS

The term "due process of law" was first used in the year 1215. This was when King John of England signed a document called the Magna Carta. The Magna Carta told the king that he had to follow certain rules. This was important because it was the first time a king was told to follow rules. Usually, the king made up the rules and punished people however he wanted. The Magna Carta made it harder for the king to punish people.

The US Constitution gives US citizens guidelines for all the laws passed.

Due Process and the Constitution

Due process became important in the United States after it became a country in 1783. In 1787, the writers of the United States Constitution took the Magna Carta's idea of following rules and made sure it was part of our laws. They also thought everyone should follow the same steps when being charged with a crime. Following these steps would

MIRANDA RIGHTS

When someone is accused of a crime and arrested, police taking the person to jail will tell him or her their rights. These rights

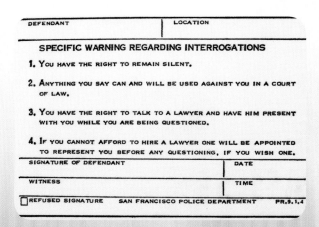

are written in the Fifth Amendment. They are often called Miranda rights or a Miranda warning. They are: the right to remain silent, the right to a lawyer, and the right to use in court anything the person says. They are named after Ernesto Miranda, a man who won a Supreme Court case in 1966 after he was not read his rights before talking about a crime with police.

"No free man shall be seized or imprisoned, or stripped of his rights or possessions ... except by the lawful judgment of his equals or by the law of the land." —Clause 39 of the Magna Carta

help people who thought they were innocent prove their innocence.

The Bill of Rights outlines the personal freedoms granted to all citizens of the United States.

Due process became important again when changes to the US Constitution were made. These changes were called amendments. They created the **Bill of Rights**. The Fifth Amendment and the Fourteenth Amendment spoke about due process.

CHRONOLOGY

Pre-1215 English Common Law establishes a set of traditions.

1215 Magna Carta is issued.

1783 The United States becomes its own country.

1787 The US Constitution is signed.

1791 The US Bill of Rights and the Fifth Amendment are passed.

1868 The Fourteenth Amendment is passed.

1966 Miranda versus Arizona court case establishes Miranda rights.

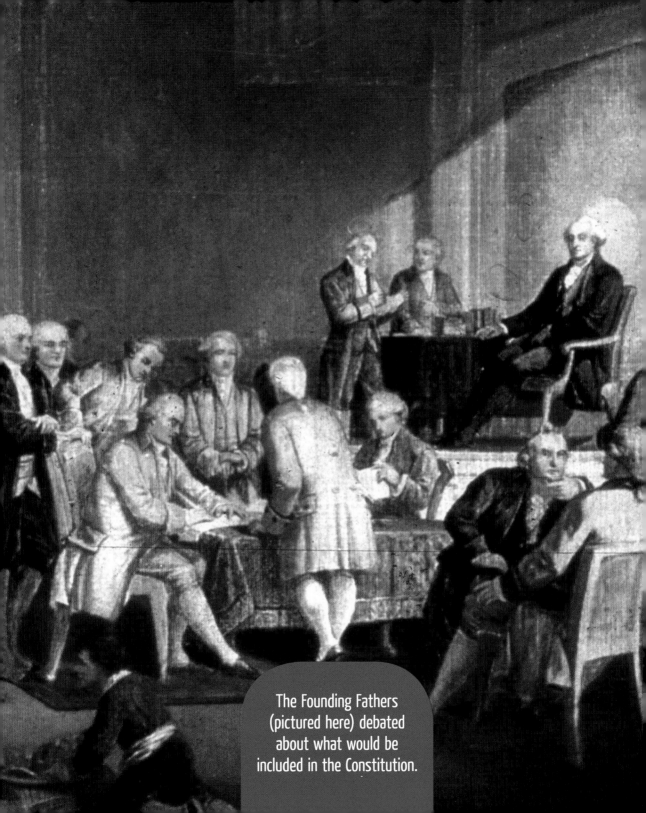

The Founding Fathers (pictured here) debated about what would be included in the Constitution.

CONSTITUTIONAL RIGHTS AND DUE PROCESS

D ue process is an important part of the US Constitution. The **Founding Fathers** thought it was important to protect citizens in the document. They did this in a few ways. One way was to create the Bill of Rights. Several amendments in the Bill of Rights talk about due process.

The justices of the Supreme Court determine if laws follow what is in the US Constitution (*pictured here*: the justices as of 2017).

Amendments

The first amendment to talk about due process is the Fifth Amendment. It says the government cannot not take away the rights of citizens without giving

THE SIXTH AMENDMENT

The Sixth Amendment describes what rights people accused of a crime have. Some of these rights include the right to a quick trial by a jury, the right to know what crime they are charged with, and the right to tell their side of the story using witnesses.

them due process. Because the government is bigger, stronger, and has more influence than citizens living in a country, it is important to give the government

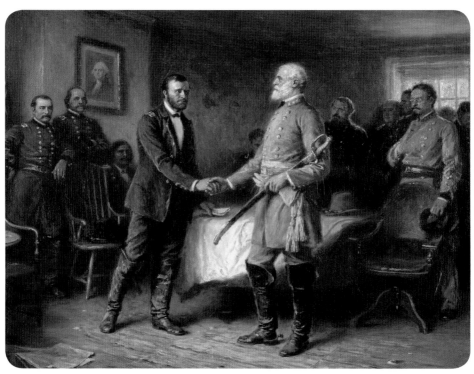

The end of the Civil War (illustrated here) helped bring about changes to the US Constitution.

rules to follow. The Founding Fathers wanted to make sure that people were protected from the government.

Other amendments came later. One of the most important amendments is the Fourteenth

Amendment. It was passed in 1868, a few years after the American Civil War. It said that individual states had to respect the same due process laws as the federal government. That meant the states could not take away a citizen's right without following due process.

The Due Process Clause

A special part of the Constitution is the Due Process Clause. It states how a person can be convicted of a

THE FOURTEENTH AMENDMENT

"All persons born or naturalized in the United States and subject to the jurisdiction thereof, are citizens of the United States and of the State wherein they reside. No State shall … deprive any person of life, liberty, or property, without due process of law."

James Madison (*below*), a Founding Father, wrote the Due Process Clause.

crime. These rules say that the government cannot simply punish someone they think committed a crime. They must prove in court that the person committed a crime.

Today, due process is still an important part of the US Constitution and can help people understand how their rights work.

Thirty-ninth Congress of the United States, at the first session, begun and held at the City of Washington, in the District of Columbia, on Mo-day the fourth day of December, one thousand eight hundred and sixty-five.

Joint Resolution proposing an amendment to the Constitution of the United States.

Be it resolved by the Senate and House of Representatives of the United States of America in Congress assembled, (two-thirds of both Houses concurring,) That the following article be proposed to the legislatures of the several States as an amendment to the Constitution of the United States, which, when ratified by three-fourths of said legislatures, shall be valid as part of the Constitution, namely:

Article XIV.

Section 1. All persons born or naturalized in the United States, and subject to the jurisdiction thereof, are citizens of the United States and of the State wherein they reside. No State shall make or enforce any law which shall abridge the privileges or immunities of citizens of the United States; nor shall any State deprive any person of life, liberty, or property, without due process of law; nor deny to any person within its jurisdiction the equal protection of the laws.

Section 2. Representatives shall be apportioned among the several States according to their respective numbers, counting the whole number of persons in each State, excluding Indians not taxed. But when the right to vote at any election for the choice of electors for President and Vice President of the United States, Representatives in Congress, the Executive and Judicial officers of a State, or the members of the Legislature thereof, is denied to any of the male inhabitants of such State, being twenty-one years of age, and citizens of the United States, or in any way abridged, except for participation in rebellion, or other crime, the basis of representation therein shall be reduced in the proportion which the

The Fourteenth Amendment was passed in 1868 to ensure all citizens had due process rights at the state level.

Due process procedures help police officers know the steps they have to take when arresting or questioning someone.

CHAPTER FOUR

USES OF DUE PROCESS TODAY

Today, due process is part of every US **legal** system. Lawyers, police officers, and judges have learned to follow it in everything they do. It is so important to the legal process that if a person is arrested and not given due process, they cannot legally be punished.

It is important to remember that due process is a right given to every citizen. That means that anyone can use it if they need to. Sometimes due process

JUDGE FRIENDLY'S DUE PROCESS LIST

Judge Henry Friendly wrote an article in 1975 that helped explain the Sixth Amendment in more current terms. This article offered more specific guidance as to how the Sixth Amendment should be applied in a modern court system. He suggested eleven parts that made up a fair trial. Some of these parts are the right to call witnesses, the right to have an attorney, and the right to have the final decision reviewed by a higher court. This article was very helpful and continues to be the standard for how trials are run today.

The Supreme Court makes their decisions at the Supreme Court Building in Washington, DC. If they decide a law doesn't follow the Constitution, the law is no longer a law.

protects the innocent. Sometimes due process proves that someone who said they were innocent is actually guilty. Due process is one of the most important parts of the law in the United States.

"As long as I have any choice, I will stay only in a country where political liberty, toleration, and equality of all citizens before the law are the rule." —Albert Einstein

Due process helps to ensure that all people are treated equally under the law.

INTERPRETING THE CONSTITUTION

The US Constitution gives a lot of rules to follow and mentions a lot of different situations. However, there is no way it could include every possible situation. Courts help make final decisions about all situations, especially those not specifically mentioned in the Constitution.

GLOSSARY

Bill of Rights A document that lists the first ten changes made to the US Constitution.

civic values Ideas that are important to and practiced by people. Examples are honesty, equality, and justice.

civil rights Actions that citizens can take that cannot be punished by the government.

discrimination When someone puts another person down because of how they look, dress, or act.

Founding Fathers The men who helped come up with rules and laws after the United States became a country.

legal The system in the United States that protects and follows all laws.

FIND OUT MORE

Books

Cheney, Lynne V. *We the People: The Story of Our Constitution*. New York: Simon & Schuster Books for Young Readers, 2012.

Rodgers, Kelly. *We the People: Civic Values in America*. Primary Source Readers. Huntington Beach, CA: Teacher Created Materials, 2014.

Website

History for Kids: The Bill of Rights

http://www.historyforkids.net/bill-of-rights.html

Video

Due Process Definition for Kids

https://www.youtube.com/watch?v=1-GNuNMbjMU

This video gives a brief definition of due process.

INDEX

Page numbers in **boldface** are illustrations. Entries in **boldface** are glossary terms.

ABOUT THE AUTHOR

Matt Bougie grew up in a small town in central Wisconsin. After graduating from St. Norbert College in De Pere, Wisconsin, he moved to Milwaukee, Wisconsin, to pursue a career. He still lives there with his girlfriend Dani and their two dogs. He works at a marketing company and as a freelance writer. In his free time, he enjoys watching sports, riding his bicycle, and reading.